the angelus & regina caeli

Meditations for Everyday Life

jared dees

praise

for the First Edition of Praying the Angelus

"Jean-François Millet's famous painting *The Angelus* captures workers of long ago stopping to pray in the field. In a modern context, Jared Dees leads busy people to appreciate this biblically-rooted devotion and, through guided meditations, makes this ancient prayer of the Church come beautifully alive once again."

Most Rev. Joseph E. Kurtz
Archbishop of Louisville
Former president of the United States Conference of
Catholic Bishops

"This book is a necessary read for those seeking to develop an interior life based around the discipline of prayer. With the gift of a teacher, Dees treats the Angelus not simply as an ancient practice but as a school of prayer for the modern person."

Timothy O'Malley
Director of the Notre Dame Center for Liturgy

"Excellent, excellent work by Jared Dees. The best explanation of the Angelus I've seen yet, expanded with background, solid Catholic teachings, and personal anecdotes that bring this traditional Catholic devotion to life. This really is a keeper!"

Marge Fenelon
Author of *Our Lady, Undoer of Knots*

For more information, visit jareddees.com.

Paperback: ISBN 978-1-954135-08-6
eBook: ISBN 978-1-954135-09-3

Second Edition. Previously published before substantial changes as *Praying the Angelus* (©2017).

contents

the angelus

V. The Angel of the Lord declared unto Mary.
R. And she conceived of the Holy Spirit.
Hail Mary, full of grace, the Lord is with thee;
Blessed art thou among women and blessed is the
fruit of thy womb, Jesus. Holy Mary, Mother of God,
pray for us sinners, now and at the hour of our
death.

V. Behold the handmaid of the Lord.
R. Be it done to me according to thy word.
Hail Mary ...

V. And the Word was made flesh.
R. And dwelt among us.
Hail Mary ...

V. Pray for us, O holy Mother of God.
R. That we may be made worthy of the promises of
Christ.

Let us pray:
Pour forth, we beseech thee, O Lord, thy grace into
our hearts, that we, to whom the Incarnation of
Christ, thy Son, was made known by the message of
an angel, may by his Passion and Cross be brought to
the glory of his Resurrection. Through the same
Christ our Lord. Amen.

the regina caeli

Queen of Heaven, rejoice, alleluia.
For he, whom you did merit to bear, alleluia.
Has risen as he said, alleluia.
Pray for us to God, alleluia.

V. Rejoice and be glad, O Virgin Mary, alleluia.
R. For the Lord is truly risen, alleluia.

Let us pray:
O God, who gave joy to the world through the
Resurrection of thy Son, our Lord Jesus Christ, grant,
we beseech thee, that through the intercession of the
Virgin Mary, his Mother, we may obtain the joys of
everlasting life. Through the same Christ our Lord.
Amen.

the angelus & regina caeli

introduction

More than two thousand years ago an angel visited a young, unmarried woman unexpectedly and announced she would become the Mother of God. As a humble handmaid, she said yes and let the Holy Spirit come upon her. That day our God took on human flesh and grace has poured forth into the world ever since.

In the Angelus Prayer we remember and meditate on this spectacular event. The Angelus is a daily Catholic devotion focused on the Incarnation of Christ. The call to pray the Angelus—still ringing in many church bell towers throughout the world—occurs three times each day, at dawn, midday, and at dusk. At 6:00 a.m., noon, and 6:00 p.m., Catholics around the world stop what they are doing and remind themselves of the presence of God in the world.

In both practice and content, the Angelus

meets us exactly where we need God's grace the most. Our culture escalates in us a desire to take control of our lives and determine our own destinies. Many of us are so focused on productivity that almost every hour of every day is scheduled and dedicated to accomplishing something. Work, for many people, is no longer contained within a nine-to-five workday: it follows us home on our devices. Those devices distract us continually, pulling us away from genuine interaction with the people around us at any given moment.

Praying the Angelus, on the other hand, reminds us to dedicate our time, our work, and our lives back to God. Each time we pray the Angelus, we stop what we are doing and pray; we reorient our lives and our time toward God, the source of our lives and the inspiration for our work. In pausing to consecrate time back to God and rededicate our lives to him, we recognize that our life and our work are gifts that he has given to us and that we give back in return.

During the Easter season we recognize the Resurrection as the greatest gift from God. Instead of praying the Angelus, we recite the words of the Regina Caeli (or "Regina Coeli"). This prayer recognizes the Virgin Mary, Mother of God, as the Queen of Heaven. We pray the Regina Caeli to share with her the great joy of the Resurrection and ask for her intercession as we also look forward to the joy we hope to experience with her Son in everlasting life.

Praying the words of the Angelus and the Regina Caeli can lead us to meditate on our daily lives. We can view our work and our calling through the lens of Mary's response to God's call through the angel Gabriel. We can reflect on our own response to God's call to us each day. We can offer up our lives and increase our awareness of the presence of God's Word in our lives and in our relationships with others. We can remind ourselves each day, as we worry about our time, that indeed our time here is limited and that we are meant for eternity.

In his apostolic exhortation *Verbum Domini*, Pope Benedict XVI summarized best the purpose of the Angelus: "This prayer, simple yet profound, allows us 'to commemorate daily the mystery of the Incarnate Word.' It is only right that the People of God, families and communities of consecrated persons, be faithful to this Marian prayer traditionally recited at sunrise, midday and sunset. In the Angelus we ask God to grant that, through Mary's intercession, we may imitate her in doing his will and in welcoming his word into our lives. This practice can help us to grow in an authentic love for the mystery of the Incarnation."[1]

Praying the Angelus is an act of openness to God's will. By stopping whatever we are doing and shifting our focus to him, we open our lives to his will and elevate its importance above our own desires of the moment. We can find great peace in our busy lives when we stop and remember that we are put here on earth to do God's will. Praying the Angelus three times each day reminds us that our lives are not our own. They are gifts, and we ask God for the grace to use them as he wishes—in ways we might never imagine on our own.

the basics

Let's start with the basics. If someone were to ask you about the Angelus and Regina Caeli, here is what you might say:

the time

We pray the Angelus every day at three times a day: 6:00 a.m., noon, and 6:00 p.m. We may still hear bells ring in Catholic churches at each of these times to remind us to pray.

the name

The name of the Angelus is taken from the its first words in Latin: *Angelus Domini nuntiavit Mariae*, which means "The Angel of the Lord declared unto Mary." These words refer to the visit of the Angel Gabriel to Mary at the Annunciation. Likewise, the name of the Regina Caeli is from the opening Latin words of the prayer: *Regina Caeli, laetare, alleluia*, which means "Queen of Heaven, rejoice, alleluia."

the purpose of the angelus

The Angelus is an invitation to meditate on the Incarnation of Jesus Christ. The words are taken from the Gospel of Luke's account of the Annunciation and the opening of the Gospel of John, which describes Jesus as the Word made flesh. We also pray three Hail Marys during the Angelus, which is another prayer inspired by the Annunciation in Luke 1.

the origin of the angelus

The Angelus originated with a practice of praying the Hail Mary three times. This practice was often initiated by the ringing of the church bells. Eventually the full words of the Angelus were recited along with the three Hail Marys. It became a way for lay Catholics to practice prayer throughout the day in solidarity with the monks and nuns who prayed the Liturgy of the Hours many times throughout the day.

the painting

The Angelus is also recognized as one of the most famous paintings of people praying. In 1857 and 1859, French painter Jean-François Millet created an oil painting of two praying peasants with a church steeple in the background.

the purpose of the regina caeli

During the Easter season we recite the Regina Caeli instead of the Angelus three times each day. Filled with the many recitations of "Alleluia," the Regina Caeli celebrates the joy of the Resurrection with Virgin Mary as Queen of Heaven.

the origin of the regina caeli

In 1742 the Pope asked the Church to pray the Regina Caeli instead of the Angelus during Easter, but the words of the prayer actually predate the formation of the Angelus as far back as the sixth century. According to legend, Pope Gregory the Great heard an angel singing some of the words of the Regina Caeli during an epidemic in Rome.

how to pray the angelus & regina caeli

Praying the Angelus is very simple. It takes only a couple of minutes, three times a day. At three specific times each day—dawn (six o'clock in the morning), midday (noon), and dusk (six o'clock in the evening) Catholics around the world stop whatever they are doing and recite the Angelus alone or in groups.

The prayer is anchored by three Hail Marys that are prayed after three paired scripture-based affirmations honoring the Annunciation and the Incarnation. The fourth pair of lines is prayer for Mary's intercession. These four pairs each comprise a versicle (V.) and a response (R.), which can be either prayed by an individual or split between a leader who recites the versicle, or the call, and a group who give the response. The Angelus concludes with a petition that God pour his grace into our daily lives.

During the fifty days of Easter, we set aside the Angelus to meditate and pray on the Regina Caeli, a prayer focused on the joy of the Resurrection of Jesus Christ and the hope that we may share with him in everlasting life.

Learning the words of the Angelus and Regina Caeli by heart takes a little time, but learning to integrate these prayers into your daily routine is by far the more challenging task. Today, we commonly live and work far from church bells tolling, reminding us to pray, and so we must set digital reminders on our phones, computers, or clocks. With these reminders in place, we simply need to commit to praying no matter what. We must decide that when that reminder pops up, we will drop everything and pray.

Choosing to pray the Angelus is not as easy as you might think. It takes courage to pray in public and discipline to pray it consistently even when you feel it has not made any impact on your life. Most days—indeed three times every day—you will have to choose to stop what you're doing—no matter what—and pray the Angelus. This is the case for everyone who practices a disciplined devotional life. No matter who you are, whether a busy parent or a celibate monk, you will have to make the daily decision to continue the practice.

It never becomes easy, but it can change your life through discipline, perseverance, and openness to God's grace.

the origin and history

The Angelus developed out of our religious ancestors' ardent desire both to honor the role of the Virgin Mary in salvation history and to practice a devotion to remember and experience the grace of the Incarnation.

When we pray the Angelus, we are united not only with others who pray this prayer each day, but with countless of the faithful over the centuries who have dedicated short moments of their day in unison with the whole Church to acknowledge and honor God's presence here on earth. The origin and history of the Angelus reveal that the unity and communion of our Church have their foundation in the Incarnation. God became man and dwelt among us during his earthly life not only to inspire us but also to unite us. Today, we rediscover this unity by meditating on the Incarnation each time we pray the Angelus alone or in a group.

Here are some of the key developments in the history of the Angelus and Regina Caeli devotions:

the ave maria (or hail mary)

Christian devotion to the Virgin Mary can be traced back to the earliest history of the Church. There are instances in the gospels that place particular emphasis on the Virgin Mary's importance in salvation: Jesus presents his mother to the beloved disciple from the Cross in the Gospel of John (19:26). Mary is present during Pentecost in the book of Acts (1:14). But it is Luke's account of the Annunciation, of course, that establishes Mary's place in the devotional life of the Church. From this story comes a wellspring of prayers entrusting the lives of the faithful to the aid of the Mother of God.

In the second century, St. Irenaeus took what St. Paul wrote about Christ as the Last (New) Adam (1 Cor 15:45) and showed that we could also look to Mary as the New Eve: "It was the knot of Eve's disobedience that was loosed by the obedience of Mary. For what the Virgin Eve had bound fast through unbelief, the Virgin Mary set free through faith."[2] This quotation shows that early Christians recognized Mary had an important place within salvation history.

As time went on, including Mary in prayer became more common. The fourth-century saint Basil the Great is credited with writing, "O sinner, be not discouraged, but have recourse to Mary in all your necessities. Call her to your assistance, for such is the divine will that she should help in every kind of necessity." What words did Christians use through the ages in their recourse to Mary? They looked to the Gospel of Luke for inspiration for a prayer.

The Ave Maria, known in English as the Hail Mary, took on a devotional formula sometime in the eleventh century. It first echoes the words of the angel Gabriel during the Annunciation. His words praise Mary as "full of grace" and offer assurance that "the Lord is with" her (see Lk 1:28). These words are followed by the words Elizabeth said to Mary at the Visitation: "Blessed are you among women and blessed is the fruit of your womb Jesus" (see Lk 1:42). The second half of the Hail Mary, our petition for her prayers, was added around the time of the Council of Trent in the sixteenth century and is not drawn directly from scripture.

the power of three

The three Hail Marys form the backbone of the Angelus prayer and also point to its beginning. During the Middle Ages, reciting the Hail Mary become commonplace; what is more, the practice of saying it three times became more and more prominent. The triple Hail Mary is often traced back to St. Anthony of Padua, who in the thirteenth century, taught his followers to "seek refuge in Mary . . . [who] provides shelter and strength for the sinner." Later in the thirteenth century, it is said that Our Lady appeared to St. Mechtilde, who called on Mary to assist her in her hour of death. Mary said to her, "I will, certainly, but I also want you to say three special Hail Marys to me every day."

Around the same time, Our Lady is said to have appeared to St. Gertrude the Great, saying, "To any soul who faithfully prays three Hail Marys, I will appear at the hour of death in splendor so extraordinary that it will fill the soul with heavenly consolation." The triple Hail Mary continued to be prayed and recommended by many other saints from the Middle Ages down through modern times, including St. Bonaventure, St. Stanislaus Kostka, St. Louis de Montfort, St. Gerard Majella, St. Alphonsus Liguori, and St. Josemaría Escrivá.

In the fourteenth century, the triple Hail Mary became a formal practice following Compline—the final daily prayer of the Divine Office or Liturgy of the Hours—in Rome. This action paved the way for this short devotion to take on a widespread appeal. Historical evidence suggests that the triple Hail Mary was said by the laypeople, who were illiterate and unable to follow along with much of the Office. At first, the recitation of the triple Hail Mary was associated only with Compline, but eventually the practice spread to the morning hour and later to noon as well.

adding the angelus

Sometime in the sixteenth century, the full text of the Angelus appeared in Catholic devotional books. Its earliest known appearance was in the *Little Office of the Blessed Virgin* in 1566. St. Peter Canisius published it in his *Catholic's Manual* in 1588. An ardent proponent of praying the Rosary, Canisius is also credited with adding the petition "Holy Mary, Mother of God, pray for us sinners" to the Hail Mary.

Aside from these early citations, not much more is known about the development and practice of the Angelus, since it was a devotional practice and not a part of Eucharistic liturgies. No one knows for sure who first composed the prayer. The words, of course, are grounded in scripture (see Lk 1, Jn 1), but we will never know who first assembled them together with the three Hail Marys and concluding prayers. We do know, however, that the practice grew and became widespread in the seventeenth century and has continued until today.

the history of the regina caeli

In 1742, Pope Benedict XIV asked that the Regina Caeli be prayed in place of the Angelus during the season of Easter (Easter Vigil to Pentecost Sunday). While this is a more recent alteration in the devotion, the Regina Caeli prayer itself actually predates the current form of the Angelus.

While the authorship of the prayer is uncertain, it is believed that Pope Gregory V introduced the Regina Caeli in the tenth century. Legend has it, though, that the prayer is much more ancient. As the story goes, another Pope Gregory, the sixth-century saint Gregory the Great, heard an angel singing the words of the Regina Caeli as he led a procession past the Mausoleum of Hadrian near St. Peter's Basilica during a time of extreme epidemic. The pope replied to the angel, *"Ora pro nobis Deum, alleluia!"* or "Pray for us to God, alleluia!"—part of the text of the Regina Caeli prayer we know today. The angel responded to the pope's plea by ending the pestilence that plagued the city. This is also one of the legends that explain the renaming of the Mausoleum of Hadrian to *Castel Sant'Angelo* (Castle of the Holy Angel) and the nearby bridge to *Ponte Sant'Angelo* (Bridge of the Holy Angel).

Today, Catholics continue to pray the Regina Caeli in place of the Angelus during the season of Easter. Like the Angelus, it is a prayer that holds both Mary and heavenly angels at its core. Instead of focusing on the Annunciation and the Incarnation, however, this prayer focuses on the Resurrection and the joy of salvation. In this way, the two prayers act as bookends to our experience of Christ: he dwelt among us, uniting us together within his Church here on earth, and now he leads us to unity with him in everlasting life.

the angelus bells

To fully understand the tradition and history of the Angelus, however, one must know a little bit about the use of bells in Church history. Prior to the wide availability of clocks and watches, church bells had a couple of very practical purposes. The bells rang to announce the beginning of Mass, as they still do for most churches today. In earlier times, though, they were also used, especially in monasteries, to announce the times to pray the Divine Office. Throughout the Middle Ages, bells were rung even in parish churches for the morning Matins prayer and evening Vespers. As the practice of praying the triple Hail Mary and then the Angelus became more common, the bells became the means of calling both religious and laypeople to join together in prayer, no matter where they happened to be when they heard the tolling.

The bells may reveal more about the history of praying the triple Hail Mary and the Angelus than official Church texts and prayer books do. As early as the thirteenth century, church bells bore an inscription of the Ave Maria. While some of these bells were dedicated to Mary, others were dedicated to St. Gabriel the Archangel and used to announce the Angelus each day.

What better symbol could we have for the Incarnation of God than the bell? Think about it. If you are within hearing distance of a church bell tower, you have an almost constant reminder that you are always in the presence of God.

Ernest Hemingway wrote a book with bells in the title that popularized a poem by John Donne. The poem reads:

No man is an island
Entire of itself . . .
Because I am involved in mankind.
And therefore never send to know
For whom the bell tolls; It tolls for thee.[3]

Church bells toll for thee. They toll for all of us. While some of us now respond to the bells one, two, or three times each day to pray the Angelus or Regina Caeli, all of us can recognize in those bells a reminder of our unity no matter where we stand because we all hear them. The bells are also a reminder to us that Christ is present in the Blessed Sacrament in a church nearby. The presence of God is heard and felt through the beckoning toll of the bells.

why pray the angelus & regina caeli today

In my experience and the experience of many who pray the Angelus each day, there are many spiritual fruits. It is a discipline that takes time and effort to develop, but God will pour out many graces to those who take up the devotion.

Grace is the gift of God to share in his very life. When we dedicate our time to praying the Angelus and Regina Caeli, we mutually exchange gifts with God. Among these graces include:

1. The gift of repetition.
2. The gift of time.
3. The gift of service.
4. The gift of patience.
5. The gift of joy.

Let's look at each of these lessons in greater detail. I hope that in reading this you will be convinced (if you haven't been already) to take up this practice of praying the Angelus and come to understand these lessons in your heart as well as your mind.

the gift of repetition

Repetition is a powerful way to change the way you think and act. When we recite a prayer over and over again, the words can spill over into our desires and actions. After hundreds and thousands of recitations of "be it done unto me according to thy word," you start to actually accept and welcome God's will in your life. After hundreds and thousands of affirmations that "the Word was made flesh and dwelt among us," you start to comprehend God's incredible gift of his presence among us today.

The repetition of the prayer to the Mother of God enables you to take comfort in Mary's intercession. The persistent petition for God's grace opens our hearts to welcome God's gifts in our lives.

This insight won't come in an instant; instead it will most likely be revealed over time. The words of the prayers will be burned into your psyche offering constant comfort and motivation to do God's will.

the gift of time

Have you heard this before: "we just don't have enough time"? There are not enough hours in the day. There's too much to do and not enough time. Time is something we want all to ourselves so that we can accomplish the many things we feel we need to do.

The stress of not completing these projects can be overwhelming, so we begin to get anxious. The stress piles up and we easily give in to anger. As others infringe on our "personal" time, we begin to resent them. We want our time to be our own and no one else's.

The Angelus, of course, is a prayer we say at specific times during the day. We do not recite the words whenever we want. Three specific times a day, we stop whatever we are working on wherever we are working on it and recite the prayer in unison with others. This practice is in opposition to the desire for ownership over time. To stop and pray at specific times each day is to give those times back to God.

Angelus time is a sacrifice. It is often difficult. You may be in the middle of something truly important, but force yourself to stop and pray. This is truly a great way to show God that we know the time he has given us is a gift and that we choose to give it back to him.

Whether you are out in public or in a private place, stopping whatever you think is important in that moment and remembering that every moment is a gift from God is liberating. It frees you from being enslaved by work and opens you up to feelings of gratitude and appreciation for God's presence in your life.

the gift of service

Our obsession with work extends beyond time. Our tasks, to-dos, and projects can become obsessions in themselves. There is a point at which our ambition and pursuit of even the boldest of callings overcomes our ability to see the needs of those around us. If we are not careful, we can prioritize our to-do lists over the people who really need us. Even if we would never say our work is more important than our family or friends, our actions and the way we relate to those we love often tell a different story.

We often hear the term "work-life balance" used in association with the workaholic culture we live in today. The idea is that we can manage our lives as a balancing of priorities between work and personal life (family, hobbies, leisure, health, religion, etc.). Today, with work accessible wherever we go through our phones and computers, it is all too easy for pressing work projects to intrude on personal time around the clock. Balance has never been harder to achieve each day.

Praying the Angelus trains us little by little to be self-giving, humble, and holy. It slowly opens us up to God's grace within our hearts that transforms us and makes us into saints. We pray and remind ourselves daily to be servants and offer up our time as a gift for God and others.

The Angelus reminds us where that creative force comes from: "And she conceived of the Holy Spirit." It is by the power of the Holy Spirit that we bring life to the work we do today. Unfortunately, our compulsion toward producing too often causes us to see our work only as responsibility. We feel we must accomplish the work at hand. We feel as though everything is riding on us. But the felt urgency to respond to the latest e-mail right away—or the world might just come undone—is a fallacy. The world does not rest on any one person's shoulders. The Angelus reminds us that all of our work is done through the power of the Holy Spirit and that we would be wise to recognize our work as a gift for others.

Mary's response to God's call also shows us a different mode of relating to our work by expressing a reality and vocation that we all share with her: we are all handmaids (or servants), and work is an expression of service.

We serve God, of course, by doing his will, but we also serve others with our creative work. Work creates value for others and is always at the service of others. Taking on the mentality of a servant—rather than an employee demanding reward and payment—transforms the way we look at our work. Once we see work as an act of service, it is hard to justify focusing on work itself rather than on serving the people nearest to us.

The famous painting by Jean-François Millet called *The Angelus* expresses the proper relationship between work and God so beautifully. The two farmers have set their tools on the ground and bow their heads in prayer. The expansive field behind them clearly requires more work than they can possibly accomplish in a day. Yet they stop everything, set aside their work, and pray to God. The Angelus can conform us to this image so that we, too, can understand our work as a purposeful gift of service to God and to others.

the gift of patience

When most people sit down to pray, they ask God to give them answers and expect to hear or see something in response. We've all turned to God when faced with a big decision—what career path to take, what college to choose, whether we are called to a religious vocation, or how to choose between two good choices (or bad choices). We pray about our needs and expect God to help us find an answer through some act of divine revelation. In some ways, seeking God's guidance in this way is like praying for an angel to come and declare to us what we must do in life.

In praying the Angelus, we meditate on an angel's unexpected visit to Mary, an event that Mary didn't plan or pray for. The angel did not bring her the answer to a question about her vocation that she had been mulling over for weeks; she already had her life all figured out. Rather, God made his will known unexpectedly, and Mary responded in humility, turning away from the vocation she likely thought she had discerned.

Praying the Angelus, therefore, strengthens our practice of humility and openness to God's unexpected plans for us. The purpose of the prayer is not to bring before God our difficult life questions. Instead, it is a practice of openness and patience. We recognize that regardless of what we hope will occur in our lives, God has a plan. Just as he did with Mary, he may reveal a plan to us that is quite unexpected.

Like the Virgin Mary, we who pray the Angelus wait in the hope that God's will be done through us. Through this daily, repetitive devotion, we begin over time to see his will unfold before us. Like Mary, we witness God's presence and work in our day-to-day lives through the good gifts he has given to us. When we take a few minutes each day to remind ourselves of God's presence in our lives, we find clarity not through long, introspective discernment but through the fluid reception of the day's events as they transpire. We come to recognize, by stopping everything and praying at the designated times each day, that God is working in our lives in unexpected ways.

the gift of joy

Through both the discipline and the content of the prayer, the Angelus redirects our hearts and minds toward God. By intentionally interrupting whatever we are doing when it is time to pray the Angelus, we grow increasingly aware that no matter what we are doing, God is present. He is not distant and uninvolved in the world today. He is present and his Spirit can be felt within us and all around us. God is the center of our existence and is ultimately more important than any big or little activity in which we are engaged when the Angelus bell tolls.

What is the fruit of this practice in our day-to-day lives? The answer can be found most clearly in the Regina Caeli. The message of the Regina Caeli is a message of joy. We join the Virgin Mary, Mother of God, Queen of Heaven, in rejoicing over the Resurrection of her son.

How great and wonderful it is! Is there anything else in this world that matters when compared to this awesome gift of new life? Despite so much doubt and despair in the world, we can rejoice in knowing that, because of the Resurrection, even death's power over us has been shattered. We have been set free.

A brief look at the lives of Catholic saints reveals people of great joy, especially in difficult circumstances. The joy of the saints has almost always come with struggle and reliance on the assistance of the Lord. Mary herself experienced great sorrow at the suffering and death of her son, yet we can barely fathom the great joy she has in his Resurrection. When we likewise make the small sacrifice of our time in prayer, we experience a taste of the great joy of heaven.

In commitment to the consistent practice of praying the Angelus and the Regina Caeli, we find joy. We find joy in setting aside our will and the consequent openness to God's plans for us. We find joy in the gifts of God's presence in our lives and in the grace given to us throughout each and every day. We find joy in our newfound ability to recognize and receive that grace and in accepting our responsibility to proclaim our joy to the world in which we dwell.

The meditations that follow will help the Angelus and Regina Caeli take on new meaning each time you pray. I hope these words will inspire in you the desire to let the grace that God has poured into your heart ignite both a passion for seeking his will and perpetual gratitude for all that he has given you. May we find unity in this common practice and joy in meeting one day in the glory of the Resurrection.

angelus
meditations

In the second and third parts of this book, you will find brief reflections that are meant to inspire personal meditation on each phrase of the Angelus and the Regina Caeli. These may be used as weekly reflections throughout the year or read each day and recalled as you pray. You can also read them at your own pace and in isolation of the daily practice. My hope is that these reflections, whether read intermittently, all at once, or in bits and pieces, will inspire deeper meditation on how the words that you pray make an impact at this particular moment in your life. Returning to the meditations will foster a deeper understanding of each phrase and, more importantly, a deeper grasp of the meaning that these phrases have for each day.

the angelus

V. The Angel of the Lord declared unto Mary.
R. And she conceived of the Holy Spirit.
Hail Mary, full of grace, the Lord is with thee;
Blessed art thou among women and blessed is the
fruit of thy womb, Jesus. Holy Mary, Mother of God,
pray for us sinners, now and at the hour of our
death.

V. Behold the handmaid of the Lord.
R. Be it done to me according to thy word.
Hail Mary . . .

V. And the Word was made flesh.
R. And dwelt among us.
Hail Mary . . .

V. Pray for us, O holy Mother of God.
R. That we may be made worthy of the promises of
Christ.

Let us pray:
Pour forth, we beseech thee, O Lord, thy grace into
our hearts, that we, to whom the Incarnation of
Christ, thy Son, was made known by the message of
an angel, may by his Passion and Cross be brought to
the glory of his Resurrection. Through the same
Christ our Lord. Amen.

the angel of the lord declared unto mary

images of angels

When you think of angels, what is the first thing that comes to your mind? For many of us it is an image of a half-dozen plump babies with wings smiling down from their clouds in heaven. They are cute and adorable (but—let's be honest—also a little bit creepy).

If not babies, you probably pull up an image of a winged adult clothed in white. Think about that image for a moment. Would you describe paintings of Michael and Gabriel as feminine or masculine? Do they appear in your mind almost like cartoon princesses? Most people's version even of the celestial warrior Michael the Archangel has the face of someone who would not hurt a fly.

After seeing countless depictions of angels as babies or fairy princesses, we may lose our understanding of an important characteristic of God's messengers: they inspire fear. When Mary sees

Gabriel for the first time, she is frightened. The angel has to comfort her, telling her not to be afraid. In fact, this is what angels do throughout the Bible whenever they appear to people for the first time.

When the angel declared God's will for Mary, she could not have taken it lightly. Yet she listened and accepted God's will that she would conceive his son despite all the fears that must have come with her acceptance of that responsibility. Likewise, we should never expect God to communicate his will for us in ways that do not frighten us at least a little. Coming to an understanding of God's will for our lives is almost always fear-inducing whether it is perceived as good or bad. Are you afraid of what God might be calling you to be and do? This just might be that angel to be feared in your own life.

meditation

Picture in your mind an image of an angel. What does the angel look like? Is this an angel that would inspire fear such as Mary experienced? Reimagine this mental picture in such a way that you feel wonder, awe, and even fear at the sight of the angel.

good messengers

Although they don't have much in common in English, the words "angel" and "gospel" are very similar in Greek. The word "angel" in Greek is *angelos* or *aggelos*, which means "messenger." The word "gospel" descends from a direct translation into Old English of the Greek *euangelion* or *euaggelion*, which means "good message" or "good news."

Both angels and the Gospel have the same effect on the people that come in contact with them. They both bring God's message into the world and inspire a personal transformation. Whereas the angel delivered one particular good message to Mary, Mary enabled the entire world to hear the good message of salvation (the Gospel) through her son, Jesus Christ.

Today, we are God's messengers bringing the good message to the world. We carry out God's will by sharing the Good News of God's presence here in the world. May we, like the angel Gabriel, speak with confidence as we share this good message, the Gospel.

meditation

At the end of each Mass, the priest or deacon commands us to "go forth." The next time you hear those closing words, consider them a calling—just like the angel's declaration to Mary—to go out into the world and share the Good News.

the declarative

Look closely at the first chapter of the Gospel of Luke. The angel speaks in declarative sentences. A declarative sentence, you might recall from your English classes, differs from imperative sentences (commands), exclamatory sentences (strong feelings), and interrogative sentences (questions). A declarative sentence simply makes a definitive statement. The angel doesn't express strong feelings or ask questions. He doesn't give commands. He makes definitive statements about God's will and his work in the world. He has not come to Mary with a request. He has come to her bearing the good news of God's work in her life and the life of her cousin Elizabeth. He *declares* unto Mary.

How does God communicate with us? Is he asking us questions? Is he giving us commands or making requests? What if, instead, God communicates his will for us in the declarative?

When you think of a God who declares his will rather than requesting our response, you start to understand the power of the Incarnation. God is here. He is with us. He is active and working in the world whether we are aware of it or not. May we have the courage to let his will be done to us according to his Word.

meditation

Are you open to God's declaration of his will in the world, or are you resistant to the destiny he is making known? Pray for the courage to accept and welcome God's will, to let his will be done in you.

and she conceived of the holy spirit

like gods

Let's consider further the connection between Eve and Mary. Eve gave in to the temptation of the serpent and believed his false promise that she and Adam "will be like gods" (Gn 3:5). Eve craved that power and chose to take it for herself despite God's warning. With the words of the Angelus, we recall the way in which God's plan for the redemption of humanity unfolded. In an act of incredible humility, Mary let herself be overcome by God's power. She did not seek to become like a god but rather allowed God to work through her. Mary conceived, and God the Son was born into the world through the power of the Holy Spirit.

The Holy Spirit can only work in our lives when we are humble and open to God's will over our own. When we welcome the Holy Spirit into our lives, we allow God to work through us, and we find joy, peace, and fulfillment. We become in this way like

Mary, who brought Christ into the world. If we grasp, like Eve, at success, glory, and the things we selfishly want for ourselves, then we reject the work of the Holy Spirit. If we try to be godlike through our own efforts, we fail every time. Without the Holy Spirit, our life loses meaning and joy.

meditation

Make two lists. Label one list "I Want To Be in Charge" and the other list "God Is in Charge." Be honest about what areas of your life you categorize under each heading. Once you are done, think of ways you can open yourself up to moving the items on your list over to God's list.

giver of life

In the Nicene Creed we profess our faith in the Holy Spirit, "the Lord, the giver of life." This is actually the second time we mention the Spirit in the Creed. Earlier, we recall that Jesus Christ "by the Holy Spirit was incarnate of the Virgin Mary, and became man." What does this Holy Spirit do according to this proclamation of faith? The Spirit gives life.

When we echo the words of the Creed and declare the Spirit's power to create life during the Angelus, we might take the time to reflect on God's work in our world today. God, the Holy Spirit, is the giver of life. Two people, with the help of the Holy Spirit, joined in union together to form another human life. Parents never fully plan or control when conception occurs. Conception is a true gift. Couples who struggle with infertility would offer anything to receive that gift and those who experience unplanned pregnancy can likewise see conception as something they cannot fully control. It is the Spirit that gives life.

The Spirit's work in the world extends beyond conception. We use words such as "lively" and "spirited" to describe happy, passionate people. When we embrace life with joy and excitement, we are filled with the Holy Spirit. The Spirit gives us life not only at conception but also today and every day that we welcome God's presence in the world.

meditation

Are you filled with life today? Why or why not? Have the courage to open yourself up to the presence of God and the working of the Holy Spirit in the world at this moment.

creative inspiration

Artists, writers, actors, comedians, and other creative people will tell you that they do not know where inspiration comes from. They sit down and work. Sometimes inspiration strikes and something beautiful is created. Sometimes inspiration doesn't arrive and the art they make is less satisfying. Artists don't have to be religious in order to come to the realization that inspiration has a spiritual, uncontrollable nature. Knowing they are not making the art all by themselves is what can make artists humble. Art is created in unity with something deeper, something subconscious and difficult to describe. The artist's role is to humbly accept creativity and inspiration when it arrives and bring art into the world.

This is how the Holy Spirit, the giver of life, works in the world. Each day we pray the Angelus, we affirm the Spirit's power at work in the world.

Mary did not create Jesus, but neither was she merely a vessel. The Spirit worked through Mary, and Mary was filled with the grace to accept her role in bringing Christ into the world. Like Mary and like the artist, we, too, can accept the creative inspiration to bring something amazing into the world.

meditation

What act of creation is the Spirit working to create with and through you today? You do not have to be an artist or a writer to experience inspiration. What ideas and actions are you feeling compelled by but unsure if you should bring about right now? May we have courage, like Mary, to respond to God's inspiration.

behold the handmaid
of the lord

behold, be bold

We don't use the word "behold" very often in conversation; it is usually reserved for dramatic moments in movies or books. It is a word we might hear announcing something great and magnificent. "Behold" suggests something powerful and incredible and amazing. You would never use this word to draw attention to yourself in regular conversation, right?

Well, Mary does, but in a unique way. She doesn't respond to the angel with an announcement of her greatness as the future Queen of Heaven. Instead she proclaims, "Behold *the handmaid of the Lord*" (see Lk 1:38). Behold the handmaid? The very idea of beholding a humble servant is so counterintuitive. Yet Mary embraces her humility and expresses with great passion her willingness to serve God wholeheartedly. At this moment, her very soul is proclaiming the greatness not of her own gifts but of the Lord.

In artwork depicting the Annunciation, Mary is nearly always depicted with such a quiet, serene, and timid look on her face. This imagery falls short of capturing the boldness of Mary's response to the angel. To the angel's announcement in Luke 1:31 that "Behold, you will conceive in your womb and bear a son," Mary responds with that same level of authority and graceful power to "behold" her as a humble yet awe-inspiring handmaid of the Lord.

Be bold in your commitment to humility in life. Like St. Paul, boast in your weakness and dependence on God (see 2 Cor 12:1–11). Only God can create goodness in the world through you.

meditation

All of us want to have complete control over some areas of our lives, areas we resist entrusting to God. Whether it is a career path, a relationship, or a bad habit in your life that you are holding on to, be bold in your commitment to deny yourself and turn that part of your life over to God. It will be scary at first, but with this commitment and trust in God comes a great gift of peace that can never be obtained on our own.

the handmaid
cinderella

The most well-known story of a handmaid is the classic tale of Cinderella. A young lady's father dies, and she is left in the power of her evil stepmother and mean stepsisters. The king of the land throws a ball to find a bride for his son, the prince, among the young women in the kingdom. Everyone will attend except Cinderella, who is left at home to complete chores instead. Cinderella's fairy godmother comes to her aid and sends her to the ball in splendor and beauty. There she meets the prince, and they fall in love. They part as the evening ends but are reunited after the prince matches her abandoned shoe with the young lady. The handmaid becomes the royal maiden—a beautiful princess and the future queen.

Now, set Cinderella side-by-side with the Virgin Mary. Mary chooses to be a handmaid. It is through her choice to serve that she is elevated to queenship, not in this world but in the next. There's no royal ball or beautiful dress. There is no fairy godmother to transform her into someone she is not. No, she accepts who she is and proclaims the greatness of the Lord without any mention of her own gifts of beauty or stature. Mary is completely filled with the love of God and empties herself in service to him.

How do we find our happy ending? Follow Mary's path rather than Cinderella's. Don't wait for your fairy godmother to show up out of the blue and transform you into someone who will impress others. Instead, humbly embrace God's gifts in your life and vow to serve him with joy. Give thanks and offer your service to God. That is the Gospel path to the kingdom of heaven.

meditation

Are you hoping God will be your fairy godmother? Are you hoping that someday he will magically whisk all your problems away? Instead, choose service over earthly rewards, that your treasure may await you in heaven. Recognize how God has already been active in your life, and think of special ways that you can respond by serving him today.

becoming
handmaids

When we meditate upon the Angelus, we put ourselves into the stories and prayers that we recite. We imagine ourselves as Mary as we speak her words: "Behold the handmaid of the Lord. . . . Be it done unto me according to your word" (Lk 1:38). This is the only phrase of the Angelus in which we recite an actual person's words. Elsewhere, we tell parts of the Annunciation and Incarnation and pray with one another for Mary's intercession.

I find it fascinating that we take on Mary's persona in our prayerful journey to become more like her. Each time we pray her ancient words, we make them new and unite our current thoughts, troubles, hopes, dreams, and worries to them. Each time we declare ourselves to be God's handmaids and proclaim our openness to his will, we invite his presence into our lives in a new and different way—

and we are called to serve him and those around us in a new and different way.

meditation

How is God calling you to be a handmaid today? Is it as a parent or a spouse? Are you to be a handmaid to your boss at work or to the customers you serve through your job? Are you to be a handmaid in your parish? Are you to be a handmaid to the strangers you see or meet today? Or are you to be a handmaid directly to the Lord? Consider whom God is calling you to serve today, and make a special effort to serve with joy.

be it done unto me according to thy word

from fear to trust

We have such a funny relationship with God's will. Much of the time, we know what God wants us to do, but we're afraid that it won't make us happy. When we resist God's will, we almost always have other plans in place that we are afraid to lose. We want things done our way. Pope Francis addressed this state of affairs in a 2013 Twitter post: "Sometimes we know what we have to do, but we lack the courage to do it. Let us learn from Mary how to make decisions, trusting in the Lord."[4]

Mary "was greatly troubled at what was said" according to the Gospel of Luke; in fact, the angel had to comfort her: "Do not be afraid" (Lk 1:29–30). Her fear then turned to doubt: "How can this be?" she asked the angel, who reassured her that "nothing will be impossible for God" (Lk 1:34, 37).

When we have big decisions to make in life, we should expect to feel that fear at first. We should even expect, like Mary, to enter into periods of doubt about the possibility of God's will for our lives will become a reality. Ultimately, like Mary, we can turn to God in loving trust when faced with difficult choices. We may not know what the future holds, but we can be confident that God's love for us is much greater than we can understand.

meditation

Do you have any decisions that you are unsure of or afraid to act upon? You may know in your heart what you have to do. Pray for the courage to act. Decide, and place your trust in the Lord, just as Mary did.

being vs. doing

My wife tells me of a theology class she had in high school that was entirely focused on prayer. She jokes that the students used to love the days when their teacher would take them down to the chapel to just "be" in prayer. She laughs that they liked to use that "being" time as nap time. As teenagers, they just didn't see the point of it.

With our busy lives and many responsibilities, we tend to be constantly active. Every free moment, waiting in line at the grocery store or on the way to and from meetings, people are on their phones. Our work hours are packed. During our free time, we perpetually feel the need to be doing or planning something to do. If time were an empty jar, we would constantly be filling it up.

Mary shows us a different way. We don't know what she was doing when the angel appeared to her. We do know, however, that she was open to what

God planned. Mary didn't respond to the angel's declaration with a command: she didn't say "Do it" or "Make it so." She was much more receptive than that. She said "Be it done" or "May it be done" (Lk 1:38). In that phrase we find her willingness simply to let something be done. Mary, in response to the angel's message, did not feel compelled to do but chose simply to be.

meditation

Take some time today to consciously refrain from "doing" and focus on "being." Sit in silence and clear your mind of everything except Mary's simple words "Be it done." Refrain from any thoughts of working or praying harder, and just sit in God's presence for a few moments. As you go about your day, practice the art of simply being present in the midst of your busy day and resist the urge to be constantly active.

mary's fiat

Mary's words "May it be done" or "Be it done" are often referred to as her *fiat*, which is the first of these words in Latin. Mary's fiat is her submission to God's will. When we echo her words during the Angelus, we, too, submit to God's will in our lives. We model our faith after Mary's faith opening ourselves up to the will of God.

Why is Mary such a great model for faith? It all goes back to her fiat. With full trust in God, she set her will aside and let his be done. Think about the choices she had. She could have said "Let it be done later," and she could have downright refused—but she didn't. As a result, God brought redemption into the world through Mary.

God wants to bring life, peace, and goodness into this world through you, too. Are you willing to let it be done? Have the courage to echo the words of Mary and live the life God wants you to live.

meditation

Is there a fiat you need to make today? Think through your day. When have you needed or will you need to submit to God's will for your life? Pray for the strength to echo Mary's words and let it be done.

getting picked

Remember when you lined up as a kid to get picked to be on a team in gym class or during recess? It was always a nerve-wracking experience. You didn't want to get picked last because that would mean you weren't as good as the other players. You wanted to be one of the kids to be picked first, high-fiving your all-star teammates and relieved that you were good enough to be with them.

Imagine how Mary felt. She got picked. What an honor! She must have been filled with excitement and, at the same time, fear of letting God down. Despite her nervousness, though, she didn't turn down her chance to be on God's team.

God has picked you. It doesn't matter now whether you were picked first to be on the soccer team at recess as a kid. Right now, God is picking you for something. What is that something? It is likely a task or role you are good at and enjoy. What are you passionate about giving back to the world?

Are you ready to let God pick you? It is harder than it seems. We're not always willing to accept honors bestowed on us by others—even by God. Follow Mary's example. Be honored. Let God pick you. Respond by answering his call and letting it be done according to his word.

meditation

In what area of your life do you feel God is calling you to something great? Visualize God picking you like a kid waiting to join a team at recess. Look around. Who is on your team? What are you going to accomplish together?

and the word was made flesh

in the beginning

In this part of the Angelus prayer, we turn to a different gospel. We move from Luke's account of the Annunciation to the opening of the Gospel of John: "In the beginning was the Word, and the Word was with God, and the Word was God. . . . And the Word became flesh and made his dwelling among us, and we saw his glory, the glory as of the Father's only Son, full of grace and truth" (Jn 1:1, 14).

Luke shows the connection between Mary/Gabriel and the creation story with Eve/Satan, while John repeats the introductory words of Genesis ("In the beginning . . .") to connect the Incarnation with the seven-day creation story. Both gospels give us a sense of the eternity of God as well as the incredible miracle and gift that is his coming into the world as an infant.

These words from John's gospel are an important reminder of who Jesus was and is. He was not "created" in the Incarnation; he has always been and always will be. He was there in the beginning and he will be there in the end. He came into this world in flesh and blood so that we could share in his eternity.

What does that reality mean to us as we pray the Angelus? It challenges us to recognize God's presence among us. Even if we cannot "see" him in the flesh, we can still see his glory all around us through the gifts of his creation and through the relationships we have with other people.

meditation

Our God, the God who created us, became human. His gift of creation is gift enough; his gift of becoming one of us is beyond understanding. Practice gratitude today by supplementing your Angelus with a prayer of gratitude to God for creating us and for becoming one of us.

logos

John opens his gospel with an important Greek word, *Logos* (Word), which is a concept from Greek philosophy that is packed with meaning. By equating Logos with Jesus Christ, John makes an important connection between who Jesus is and the contemporary Greek conception of Logos.

Logos, in Stoic philosophy, could refer to a universal principle of reason. The word *logic* has its root in Logos. The Greeks also associated Logos with creation as the underlying force that animates the world. In that sense, God did not create the world as a potter creates a pot. Rather God is the animating force that not only made but sustains creation. Creation is not a set reality, so much as an ongoing state of existence. God is creator, and we are the created, in ongoing relationship.

What does this mean for our understanding of Christ? Why did St. John the Evangelist use the concept of Logos to open his gospel? Because it expresses the fact that even though Jesus was a human, he is not only a human. His divinity stretches beyond space and time. God is the rational force—nothing fantastical—that animates and gives us life. During the Angelus we recall that Christ became flesh, but that Incarnation didn't inhibit his eternal existence. He still dwells among us in each one of us, holding us in existence.

meditation

Consider praying for those who live according to reason alone, without faith. Find joy in the fact that the divine Logos is with them and animates them and their lives, too, even if they do not realize it.

the flesh

In St. Paul's New Testament letters, he often writes negatively about the flesh. He writes, "For I know that good does not dwell in me, that is, in my flesh. . . . For I do not do the good I want, but I do the evil I do not want" (Rom 7:18–19). We can all relate to this. We all sin. We all do things we know we should not do or fall into addictions that are hard to break. Most of these temptations and addictions have to do with bodily urges for food and sex. While not evil in themselves, temptations of the flesh can become easy doorways to sin.

We are, however, not without hope. God himself became flesh like us, sharing that same flesh that leads us so easily into sin. What an incredible gift! Yes, like St. Paul we continue to do that which we do not want, but we are not lost. Because Christ became flesh, he redeemed the flesh. Through his grace, he enables us to break free from bondage to sins of the flesh and gives us the power to rise above our temptations.

meditation

What are the temptations, addictions, and bad habits that afflict you? Recognize that our God became flesh to redeem us and save us from the evil that our flesh leads us into. As you pray the Angelus each day, ask Jesus for the grace to choose good over evil—to overcome your biggest temptations and break free from the bondage of sin.

bow your head

When we recite the Creed on Sundays, we bow our heads in unison when we say the words "and by the Holy Spirit [he] was incarnate of the Virgin Mary, and became man." Likewise, during the Angelus it is customary to bow our heads or genuflect when we say "And the Word was made flesh and dwelt among us."

Why do we bow? Bowing, of course, is a sign of humility and respect. You would bow to royalty. In some cultures, you bow as a form of greeting to show respect. You bow to your partner at the end of some traditional dances.

During an Angelus address in 1979, St. John Paul II spoke about bowing our heads. "*Inclinate capita vestra Deo!*" ("Bow your head before God!"), he began, referring to the exhortation to bow our heads on Ash Wednesday. He went on to explain the meaning of bowing the head: "Bowing the head before God is a sign of humility. Humility, however, is not identified with humiliation or resignation. It is not accompanied by faint-heartedness. On the contrary. Humility is creative submission to the power of truth and love. Humility is rejection of appearances and superficiality; it is the expression of the depth of the human spirit; it is the condition of its greatness."[5]

So, without shame or resignation, with both humility and courage, we bow before God made flesh. We recognize that our greatness comes from this place of humility. God humbled himself to become flesh like us; we humble ourselves to become like God.

meditation

Whether you are praying the Angelus right now or not, bow your head. What feelings or thoughts immediately arise? When we bow our heads, we are likely to be bowing to someone, submitting to someone. Think of that someone (God) to whom we bow. He is worthy of our submission. Take a few minutes to think about why we owe God the submission of our will, our thoughts, our very lives.

and dwelt among us

emmanuel

One of the most popular Advent and Christmas hymns is "O Come, O Come, Emmanuel." *Emmanuel* is a Hebrew word meaning "God-with-us." The song expresses our longing for God. We are in exile here without Christ; we are lonely and isolated without God.

But even today God is with us! We remind ourselves of this every time we pray these words of the Angelus: "The Word became flesh and dwelt among us." We don't have to be alone. God is present here even today. Our God is not distant and unknowable. He is present among us and working in this world even if we do not have him in the flesh anymore.

What an incredible gift that our God did not remain far off but became one of us. Through his mercy and love, God took on our flesh to be one with us. He shows his love for us by offering us his very life and his presence with us today. Though we cannot see him in the flesh, we can find comfort in knowing that he is not far off. We can experience his presence in prayer or in adoration before the Blessed Sacrament. We can recognize his presence and working in the world in each moment of our day. We can meet him in the face of strangers and friends that we encounter each day. God is here today. God is with us.

meditation

As you pray the Angelus today, think of the emotional drive behind the song "O Come, O Come, Emmanuel." Hum the tune in your head. You might even pray the words of the Angelus to that same tune. As you do, consider the hymn's desperate plea for God to be with us. At the end of your prayer, give thanks that God continues to dwell in you and in your life.

god does not hide

One of the most famous movie quotations in recent decades comes from the film *The Usual Suspects*: "The greatest trick the devil ever pulled was convincing the world he didn't exist."[6] There is a lot of truth to this claim. In fact, C. S. Lewis expressed a similar sentiment in *The Screwtape Letters*, writing as the fictional demon Screwtape: "I wonder you should ask me whether it is essential to keep the patient in ignorance of your own existence. . . . Our policy, for the moment, is to conceal ourselves."[7]

To take this idea a step further, it is safe to say that the devil has done a great deal more than conceal himself. He has completely concealed from many people the existence of any spiritual beings. Many people have accustomed themselves to the idea that since they cannot see God, angels, or demons, these spiritual beings do not exist.

Christians not only believe that God is real, but

that he took a human form and dwelt here with us on earth. People saw him, touched him, ate with him, and then shared their stories of him as witnesses to his existence. These stories were passed down from one disciple to the next and recorded in the gospels. Jesus appointed his Apostles, and they ordained bishops and priests to form a chain of witnesses to testify to God's true presence here on earth. God does not conceal himself the way the devil does. He took bodily form and dwelt among us with nothing to hide.

meditation

Imagine that you were one of the disciples at the time of Christ. Imagine that you saw Jesus with your own eyes and believed him to be the Messiah. What would you have to say about him? What would you want to communicate to the world about who he was and, in particular, who he was to you?

i am with you always

At the end of the Gospel of Matthew, Jesus leaves his disciples with some parting words: "I am with you always, until the end of the age" (Mt 28:20). In the Angelus, we proclaim that the Word was made flesh. We remind ourselves that Jesus was and is Emmanuel, "God-with-us." He was made flesh but remains with us and among us today. His parting words are a reassurance to us all that he will always be with us, dwelling among us, even if we cannot see him.

Pausing each day and reciting the words of the Angelus help remind us to look for Jesus' presence among us today. How is he with us? He is within us. He is within the people we meet and encounter each day. He permeates the natural order. He is all around us. Jesus Christ, the Word made flesh, is with us today—and the way we see the world changes day by day.

meditation

As you proceed through your day today, look for God's presence. Do you see God in the people around you? Where do you find hints of his presence in the day's events? Do you experience God's presence in the natural world?

pray for us, o holy mother of god

pray for us

So often we pray for people other than ourselves. We seek the good in and for others and appeal to God to shower his graces on them. When we need prayer and ask others to pray for us, we feel great consolation and reassurance. Hearing "I'll pray for you" from someone makes us grateful that we are not alone. United in prayer, we can find comfort not only in God's care for us but in the support of others.

At the same time, we can be limited by the number of people we confide in for prayers. We may have a large community of support, or it may be that we have only a few close friends and family that we can turn to for prayer. As Catholics, though, we can go further: we can appeal to the angels and saints to pray to God on our behalf. We may not hear a response, but we can feel confident that if we ask a humble saint for his or her help, our plea will be heard.

If this isn't reassurance enough, we can find solace in our ability to turn to the Mother of God herself to intercede for us. Read that again: the Mother of God. We can ask the Virgin Mary, the Mother of God himself, to pray for us. And she does, every time we ask. In the Angelus, we ask her to pray for us every day each time we pray. That, I hope, is some consolation in good times or bad. God's own mother is praying to her son on our behalf.

meditation

Spend some time today either during the Angelus or in between prayers to bring specific needs and prayer requests before the Mother of God. Ask for her prayers for these specific needs, and be comforted in her willingness to present them to her son, our Lord Jesus Christ.

theotokos

God has a mother. Let that sink in for a moment. He has a human mother. It is a powerful concept. The very idea threw the Church into a heated debate that led many to break into their own factions outside of the Church in the fifth century. To believe as we do that the holy, infinite, and all-powerful God would humble himself to be born as a son of a human being is nearly unbelievable. Yet that is exactly what God did. He chose a human mother here on earth to give birth to him.

In this part of the Angelus we echo that audacious Greek name for Mary, *Theotokos*, Mother of God or more literally, "God bearer." We ask her to pray for us, that we may be made worthy of her son's promises. Thanks be to God that he made this worthiness possible: our God became man so that man could become like God. Through his humility, our unworthiness can be transformed into greatness.

Our God was so humble that he took a human mother.

Think about your own mother for a moment. Whether you are close with her or not, mothers are an integral part of all our lives; we all feel—or at least we long to feel—great affection for mothers. Our God looked upon Mary with this same affection on earth and still does in heaven. This is why we seek her intercession.

meditation

In your prayers today, turn to Mary to intercede on your behalf. Ask for the strength to live out the humility of Christ and be made worthy of the promises he makes to us.

that we may be made worthy of the promises of christ

we are made worthy

We all find ourselves sometimes in situations in which we feel unworthy. This feeling of unworthiness might arise when we are asked to join a committee at our parish or our kids' school, or when we are hanging out with a new group of people or in a new social situation. We can feel unworthy while spending time with people who are more skilled than we are, more talented, more experienced, or more comfortable doing something important.

How do we get past that feeling of unworthiness? In most of these situations, we realize over time that we were actually worthy all along. We had nothing to worry about. The same goes for our relationship with God. We can take on misguided attempts to make ourselves worthy through hard work or self-effacing pain when really it is God who made us and makes us worthy. By God's grace we will continue on our way to Christ's promise of everlasting life.

meditation

In what areas and situations in your life do you feel a sense of unworthiness? Think deeply about the source of that sense of unworthiness. Is it a fear of rejection? Offer that fear to Mary, the Mother of God, to bring before the Lord on your behalf. Allow the Lord to fill the void that those feelings of unworthiness create inside of you.

pour forth, we beseech thee, o lord, thy grace into our hearts

pouring fourth

Think of all the other words we could have used in the Angelus to ask for God's grace: *give, hand over, deliver, grant, bestow, bequeath, pass out*. But none of these words quite captures the meaning of "pour forth." There is some distinct imagery here, and it has two parts.

First, we ask that grace be *poured* into our waiting hearts, not given as an object to be received. From this metaphor we learn that grace, like water, must be held in something. It cannot be carried alone like a package. It flows and fills. Grace flows into our hearts and, if we are open to God's will, is held there.

Second, grace is poured *forth* from God, not just poured. The extra word reminds us that grace has its source in God. An often used image is that of grace overflowing out of God and into us. So grace isn't just some really good thing; grace is the gift of God himself. It is his life poured forth into our lives.

Now that we have received God's grace, the pouring continues: we share that grace. It pours forth from us.

meditation

As you pour yourself a drink today—whether it is water, coffee, or something else—observe this "pouring forth" from the faucet or pitcher closely. Think now of God's grace pouring forth and filling the cup of our hearts. What will you do with that grace today? Will you let it be poured forth into the lives and hearts of others?

a heart full of grace

In the Hail Mary, we echo the words of the angel to Mary, whom he calls "full of grace." Here at the end of the Angelus we turn to God and ask that he fill us with grace as well. Notice what we ask God to fill with his grace: our hearts. This is so that we, like Mary, may love God back completely. It was God who "first loved us" (1 Jn 4:19), and we wish to love him back.

Grace is a free and undeserved gift. We hope that, filled with grace, we will be able to reciprocate with a free, completely deserved gift of our love back to God. Think about what God has done for us. He came to this earth and lived among us, he died, he rose, and he remains with us today. That is grace. That is the love of God made manifest. We ask that our hearts be so filled with grace that we can give it right back to God.

meditation

Has anyone ever given you a gift that you didn't ask for or think you deserved? You felt as though you owed that person something, right? You either gave a gift in return or sent a thank you note. Think about all the undeserved gifts you have received from God. How can you give something back to God or say thank you to him in creative ways?

that we to whom the incarnation of christ, thy son, was made known by the message of an angel

in the flesh

Paper cuts are painful. Biting your tongue can be excruciating. Stubbed toes, a stinging funny bone, chapped lips—our bodies can sustain all sorts of little annoying and painful injuries. While small, these pains can dominate our days if we let them, distracting us from what is really important in life. We can easily become complainers.

This is the bodily state that our God chose to take on for himself. God became incarnate (meaning "in the flesh") and everything that comes with it. He experienced for himself all those little, annoying pains as well as far more serious pains during his passion and death. Why? To redeem them. Every pain, no matter how annoying, finds new meaning in Christ.

How? Christ shared in that pain, too. He felt pain just as we feel pain today, no matter how great or small. Any pain, no matter how annoying, finds new meaning in Christ. Think about it. Every time we experience some bodily pain, we can recall that our God endured it, too.

meditation

Think about your body right now. Are any small wounds or pains bothering you? Try the old practice of "offering it up." It used to be a common practice among Catholic parents to tell their complaining children to "offer it up," meaning offer up your pain for the souls in purgatory. This practice helps us and those for whom we offer up our pain because we recognize that our Lord, too, experienced pains just like ours and worse. In this way, we unite our pain with his. We are not alone in the pain that comes with being fleshly creatures. God became flesh, too, and experienced that pain just like us.

from annunciation to incarnation

It is easy to focus more on the Annunciation than on the Incarnation when we pray the Angelus. The Annunciation is easy to imagine. It is much more concrete. We can picture the angel and Mary and the conversation they had with each other.

The Incarnation, however, is difficult to visualize. What do we picture in our minds when we consider the Incarnation? Do we think of baby Jesus? Do we think of grown Jesus walking around on the earth, preaching and teaching about the kingdom of God? Do we ponder the intricacies of the Trinity? Meditating on the mystery of the Incarnation can be a real challenge.

Although flesh is concrete, the Incarnation itself is an abstraction—maybe the most abstract of ideas, because the thought of God becoming man is so strange. God, who is immaterial, eternal, and omnipotent, could and would not possibly become one of us, right?

Yet he did. The Incarnation is a beautiful mystery and one worth remembering and pondering every day. While it may be easier to meditate on the Annunciation during the Angelus, we cannot forget that our real focus should remain on the Incarnation of Christ, which is what the angel came to announce.

meditation

What images come to your mind when you think of the word "Incarnation"? Write them down as they come to you. Don't try to come up with some abstract idea to ponder. Instead, focus on the specific images and thoughts that come to mind and spend time considering each one. You may find new and unexpected perspectives on the Incarnation as you do.

may by his passion and cross be brought to the glory of his resurrection

the only way to glory

How do we get to the glory of the Resurrection? The closing prayer of the Angelus reminds us that it is only through Christ's Passion and Death that we are brought to the glory of his Resurrection. That does not match up with how the rest of the world seeks glory, does it?

Many people today tend to glorify the lives of celebrities, actors, musicians, athletes, and successful businesspeople. Paparazzi feed our craving to see the latest photos or hear the latest scandal or gossip about these people. News media focus on headlines and stories that draw the attention of those who just can't wait to hear what is happening in the lives of the people we place on pedestals. Many people, whether they realize it or not, like to watch these celebrities fall. It is as if they want to be reassured that their glory is not enduring, that celebrities are really just as flawed as we are.

The Christian faith paints a different picture of glory; it tells us that glory comes only through suffering and death—death to ourselves, death to selfishness. If we seek the glory of the Resurrection rather than the glamour and glory of this world, we will find ourselves seeking to suffer on behalf of others. We will follow Christ on a path of sacrificial love—the path to true glory—the glory of the Resurrection.

meditation

What images of glory have been ingrained in your mind through popular culture? Ask yourself honestly what type of glory you have been seeking. Do you seek glory through sacrifice and death to self as the Angelus calls us to do?

reflecting on lent

We pray the Regina Caeli during Easter since it celebrates the Resurrection, but we pray the Angelus during all the other liturgical seasons. While we might say that it is especially relevant during Advent due to its focus on the Annunciation and the Incarnation, it does contain a perfect tie-in with the season of Lent.

The Angelus closes with a testimony to the Passion and Cross of Christ. After focusing on the beginning of Jesus' time here on earth, we remember his end. The mystery of the Incarnation cannot be isolated from the Passion and Death of our Lord, for it is not through the Incarnation alone that we find salvation but through Christ's saving work in the Paschal Mystery. His complete self-sacrifice leads us into grace. His humiliation opens the path to glory.

The Paschal Mystery is a traditional topic for

Lenten meditation. We remember that our God loved us so much that he died for us. We remind ourselves that the true path to glory is the path of the Cross. We give of ourselves and give up all attachments so that we can grow closer to Christ. Through this humility come joy and the glory of the Resurrection. The Angelus makes for a wonderful Lenten devotion because it promotes detachment ("Be it done unto me") and selfless serving of others ("Behold the handmaid of the Lord") and keeps our minds on the Paschal Mystery ("[may we] by his Passion and Cross be brought to the glory of his Resurrection").

meditation

Think about what you gave up during the most recent (or current) season of Lent. Relate that sacrifice to the words of the Angelus. How did you live out (or are you living out) the words we pray during the Angelus by making that sacrifice during Lent?

a suffering servant

The Old Testament prophet Isaiah wrote of the Lord's Suffering Servant: "I am honored in the sight of the Lord and my God is now my strength" (Is 49:5). As Christians, we can turn toward the Cross denying ourselves and experiencing suffering in order to find strength in God. We do not suffer for suffering's sake. When we take up our cross and serve others, we make their lives better. We make them happier and we become happier as a result.

When we follow Christ to the cross, suffering takes on new meaning. Through our own choice to suffer for others, we are strengthened and supported by God. The Angelus is a reminder of this crucial fact that God is with us especially in our suffering. We find the glory of the Resurrection through the pain of humble service. Thankfully, we are not alone. God accompanies us through this suffering.

He is our strength. We are always with and supported by God.

meditation

When we do something kind for another person, it makes that person feel good. It makes us feel good, too, especially when we aren't seeking any special recognition from others. Do something kind and unexpected for someone today, maybe even a stranger. Don't ask for anything in return. Seek glory and honor only in the eyes of the Lord, who sees what you have done even if no one else does.

through the same christ, our lord. amen.

through and through

"Through and through" is a common phrase that means "thoroughly, completely, or in every aspect." I like that. I think this phrase adds deeper meaning when we end each prayer with "through Christ, our Lord." Think of the entire world completely offered through Christ; every aspect of our lives and our world offered through Christ.

Christ is both the center and limit of our entire world.

We conclude this prayer about the Incarnation recognizing that even the prayer itself is offered through Christ. Everything we say and do exists within and through Christ. We do not reside on some distant part of the universe where God can't be found. He is here with us. He is among us. He is present.

And so we offer our prayer through him who is completely with us in every aspect of our lives.

Through him we turn over to the Father all our troubles, our worries, and our hopes.

meditation

Is there any part of your life that you feel the need to keep separate from God? Is Christ thoroughly and completely involved in every aspect of your life? Think of those areas that you can offer back to God, then offer them through Christ, your Lord.

amen

Have you ever wondered why we say the word "amen" at the end of a prayer? Sure, it serves as a nice conclusion to any prayer. It lets people know that the prayer is over. It adds a communal element so that everyone gathered can proclaim amen in unison even when we are not the ones actually saying the prayers.

But what does it mean? Jesus said amen repeatedly to introduce many of his teachings: "Amen, I say to you . . ." In Aramaic the word *aman* means "be confirmed, supported, or upheld." In Hebrew, the word *emet* means "that which is true, dependable." Some Bible translations, therefore, have Jesus introduce his teachings with "Verily, verily" or "Truly, truly." "Amen" is used to confirm the truth of and support something that is stated. In much of the southern United States it is common practice for people in Protestant (and some Catholic) congregations to shout amen in support of powerful preaching statements. Even in common conversation people will say "Amen to that" or "Amen, brother" to confirm something is true.

So, why do we say amen at the end of a prayer? We do so as an affirmation that what we have prayed together is true. In Catholic liturgies, the congregation joins in saying amen even when the priest offers a prayer on their behalf. Likewise we end the Angelus with an amen. We conclude by proclaiming that our recitation of the Angelus wasn't just a mindless ritual—it was a proclamation of a truth so deep it is worth praying again and again each day.

meditation

The next time you say amen, whether after the Angelus or after another prayer, think of the real meaning of the word. With your whole heart and mind proclaim that what you prayed is true—that you confirm and support what was said.

regina caeli meditations

the regina caeli

Queen of Heaven, rejoice, alleluia.
For he, whom you did merit to bear, alleluia.
Has risen as he said, alleluia.
Pray for us to God, alleluia.

V. Rejoice and be glad, O Virgin Mary, alleluia.
R. For the Lord is truly risen, alleluia.

Let us pray:
O God, who gave joy to the world through the
Resurrection of thy Son, our Lord Jesus Christ, grant,
we beseech thee, that through the intercession of the
Virgin Mary, his Mother, we may obtain the joys of
everlasting life. Through the same Christ our Lord.
Amen.

queen of heaven, rejoice, alleluia

the humble queen

When Jesus was asked about the place of the apostles in the kingdom of heaven, he said to them, "Whoever wishes to be great among you shall be your servant" (Mt 20:26).

This declaration makes Mary's place in the kingdom much easier for us to understand. She lived a life of complete service to and love for God. She opened herself up to God's will in her life and always stayed in the background. Look closely at her role in the gospels, in Acts, and even in the letters of the New Testament; she is rarely the focus of attention. Instead, the attention centers on her son and on the work of the Holy Spirit in this world. She lived out what she expressed in the Magnificat (see Lk 1:46–55), proclaiming the greatness of the Lord and not her own.

As we meditate on the mysteries of Christ's Resurrection and our path to everlasting life, it is good to constantly remind ourselves what kind of kingdom we are heading toward. Those who are last will be the first. If you want to be great in heaven then make yourself a servant—a handmaid—to others.

meditation

In what areas of your life do you find yourself trying to outperform or outdo others? In which areas do you seek to put others before yourself? Think for a moment about how you feel about both areas of your life. Which makes you happy? In which do you find fear and worry? Seek happiness through service to others.

coronation of mary

The final Glorious Mystery of the Rosary concentrates on the crowning of the Virgin Mary, Mother of God, as Queen of Heaven. I tend to imagine a royal celebration in her honor: the trumpets of angels blaring and lots of bright lights and heavenly bliss. It is hard not to think of medieval coronations.

Mary, though, is a queen unlike the queens of medieval times. She didn't marry into her role as queen. Instead, she gained her crown by loving and giving birth to our Lord and King, Jesus Christ.

When we think about the meaning of "regal," it is hard to associate the term with a poor peasant girl. Think back to the opening lines of the Angelus in which Mary proclaims herself a simple handmaid of the Lord—a servant of the great king. And yet it is that attitude of service to God the Father and her deep love for her son that earn her a regal place in heaven.

Mary shows us the way to enter into the kingdom: love her son with all our heart and show that love by being a servant.

meditation

When you think about a queen, what images come to mind? Now think about what you know about the life of the Virgin Mary. She shows us the way to enter into the royal kingdom of God. Consider how you can live more the way Mary did.

the queen rejoices

Some popular Marian devotions focus on the sorrows Mary suffered in her lifetime. When Mary and Joseph took the infant Jesus to the Temple to consecrate him to God, Mary met Simeon, who prophesied about her forthcoming suffering, saying, "and you yourself a sword will pierce" (Lk 2:35). This is the first of the Seven Sorrows of Mary, a traditional Catholic devotion that focuses our meditation on the meaning of this prophecy.

When we reflect on the Easter joy of the Resurrection, we do not forget the sacrifices we made during Lent to get here. That suffering—even when it has not been too burdensome—makes the joy of Easter even more satisfying. After all, Easter candy tends to taste just a little bit better than usual to those who have abstained from sweets for forty days.

Imagine the great joy Mary felt at her son's

Resurrection after her great sorrow in witnessing his suffering and death. This is the joy we call to mind in the Regina Caeli. We exhort Mary—who suffered so much pain—to rejoice again in her son's Resurrection. In proclaiming her joy, we ask her to share that joy with us as well. In memory of her sorrow, we rejoice that the Resurrection is here.

meditation

If you are meditating on this prayer during the season of Easter, think back to your forty-day Lenten journey. What did you sacrifice or give up on the way to Christ's death on the Cross? How excited were you to have once again that which you gave up?

clouds of heaven

To imagine heaven and not think of clouds is almost impossible. Classic and popular art and film have ingrained this imagery in our minds. Even the Bible mentions clouds when it describes Jesus' Ascension (Acts 1:9) and Second Coming (Mt 24:30; Rv 1:7).

Whether you enjoy flying or not, you have to admit that being in an airplane and flying above, through, and around the clouds is breathtakingly beautiful. It is hard to comprehend that what we're seeing is real—it's as if we're watching a movie outside the windows. It makes sense, then, to imagine that heaven will match and yet somehow exceed the beauty of the clouds in our skies.

We do not have to fly in planes to witness the beauty of this world. There is beauty everywhere if we take the time to stop and observe the world around us. This beauty of creation, properly appreciated, can inspire within us feelings of joy and gratitude and lead us to praise God. We may have to wait to experience the beauty of our heavenly home, but we don't have to wait to find joy in the beauty of our earthly home.

meditation

Take some time today to observe the beauty of the world around you. Go outside and experience nature. Whether the sun is shining or the rain is pouring down, thank God for the beauty around you. Through those acts of gratitude, you will open yourself up to experience the Resurrection joy we proclaim in the Regina Caeli.

finally, alleluia!

As little girls, our daughters were always sticklers about Alleluias during Lent. When a Vacation Bible School CD would play in the car with a song that had an alleluia in it, my girls would shout to us to skip to the next song before it was too late. This is because during the Lenten liturgies, the Catholic Church does not say alleluia before the Gospel nor do we sing any songs with alleluia in it. We save it for Easter. I remember one Easter Mass when my two-year-old, who was paying more attention to the ribbon in the hymnal than to what was going on at the altar, suddenly stopped in amazement during the Gospel acclamation and, pointing to the choir, shouted up at me, "Alleluia, Daddy!"

There are many times in our lives when the alleluias are set aside for a little while. We may have a bad day or bad week. We may fall into a rut at work or in a relationship. We can find ourselves just going through the motions. Yet these dips in life, these moments of dryness, will someday come to an end. At some point, we will again hear and feel that alleluia. It may require patience.

It may seem as though that time will never come, but it will. Like the surprise my daughter felt when she heard alleluia again at Mass for the first time in forty days, we, too, will find joy in life again.

meditation

Are there any areas in your life that feel empty and unexciting? Are you in a rut of some sort? Offer these parts of your life to God as you pray the Regina Caeli. Ask for the Queen of Heaven's intercession that God give you back that spirit of alleluia once again.

for he, whom you did merit to bear, alleluia

christ bearers

Of the many titles of Mary we proclaim in the Angelus and Regina Caeli, one of the most subtle is "Christ bearer." As the Mother of Christ, who is God, Mary became the Mother of God. She carried our God in her womb. She brought him along on a journey to visit her cousin Elizabeth. She bore him on the trip to Bethlehem and there gave birth to him. It didn't stop at his birth, though. She brought him with her to many other places during his childhood. Then, after he had died, risen, and ascended into heaven, she continued to bear her son in the world by the power of the Holy Spirit. She, too, was present at Pentecost. Like the Apostles, she carried forth the Spirit of Christ in the world.

Like Mary, we can bear Christ within the world. We can take him with us into everything we do in our days. We can merit our bearing of him by our humble service and ceaseless consideration of God's will in our lives. Then, through this commitment to become Christ bearers, we can rejoice with Mary and find the alleluias in our lives.

meditation

Are there any areas in your life where you find it difficult to bring Christ with you? Such areas may be where we need God the most. They can become the greatest opportunities for transformation. Find the alleluias in your life by imagining Christ with you throughout every part of this day—at work, at home, while hanging out with friends, even in the simple and mundane activities of your day.

the merits of mary

When Boy or Girl Scouts accomplish certain goals, they earn merit badges. The badges are sewn onto vests displaying every badge they have earned. These accomplishments become a part of their identity as scouts.

An interesting analogy can be made here about our spiritual merit as it relates to God and our salvation. No one has any merit at all apart from God. God is like the vest. Any merit we may have is linked to our relationship with him. Just as the merit badge is sewn onto the vest, our merit is linked to God.

God's infinite love for us far outweighs any action we could possibly take to merit that love from him. He bestows his grace on us despite our faults. That grace—God's sharing of his life with us— enables us to experience his love and extend that love to others. God's grace, in other words, is the source of any merit we could possess. Without that link to God, the merit is as meaningless as an unattached merit badge that is lost or tucked away in a drawer somewhere.

In the Regina Caeli, we address Mary as the one who "did merit to bear" Jesus Christ. Is there any better description of spiritual merit than this? Overcome by the power of the Holy Spirit, Mary became the Mother of God. Because of her faith and fullness of grace, she did merit to bear the Son of God to the world.

Maybe merit comes down not so much to what we can do through our own hard work, but to what God can do through us. Mary, therefore, merited to bear Jesus because she allowed God to work through her. We venerate her because of God's great work in and through her.

meditation

Reflect on your own merit as a future Christian saint. Don't think of all your hard work to be holy or your extra efforts to pray and do good works. Think instead of the great gift of God's grace in your life. How have you been touched by his love? How has he been with you, guiding and sustaining you in your daily life?

putting the angelus in perspective

If the two prayers weren't linked by long tradition, you could easily miss the connection between our Easter Regina Caeli and the Angelus. There is good reason for the pairing. The Regina Caeli in many ways puts our Angelus meditation on the Annunciation and Incarnation into perspective. The Annunciation isn't complete without the Resurrection.

Mary, the Queen of Heaven, is the Mother of God. Her merit is due to her deeply intimate relationship with God. She is God's mother. It sounds almost blasphemous to say, but it is true. Mary is the Mother of God—of the One who is risen from the dead, the One who conquered death itself. The Resurrection only happened because a lowly handmaid said yes to an angel announcing the virgin birth of a son.

We don't think about Christmas very often

during the season of Easter. Maybe we should. The seasons of Advent and Christmas—seasons to remember the preparation for and event of the birth of Christ—find completion in the season of Easter— a season to celebrate the Resurrection of Christ and our new birth. In the same way, the Angelus finds completion in the Regina Caeli.

meditation

As you pray the Regina Caeli today, remember the Annunciation and the birth of Christ. Those stories find their fulfillment in the joys of the Easter Resurrection. How do they take on new meaning in the context of the Resurrection?

no hail marys

The contrast between praying the Angelus and praying the Regina Caeli is probably felt most clearly in the lack of the triple Hail Marys that have been at the core of the Angelus practice for centuries. In the Regina Caeli, we repeat other words much more fitting for the season of Easter.

We repeat the word "alleluia" six times and the word "joy" four times, five if you translate the Latin word *gaude* as "be joyful" instead of "be glad." Alleluia is a word that expresses our praise to God. It isn't something we say simply because we like God a lot or think he is really great. We praise God with our alleluias because of his great work: he has risen from the dead and saved us from our sins. The Resurrection can make us joyful. Out of that joy, we give praise to God.

While you may miss the prayerful reminders of the Incarnation in the Hail Marys, our frequent repetition of "alleluia" and "rejoice" in the Regina Caeli during this Easter season enables us to praise God in a different way. Not only has he come into the world and dwelt among us, he has died just as we will die and gone on to conquer death. This is certainly something to praise him for.

meditation

Since you won't pray the Hail Mary during your Easter season Regina Caeli, take some time today to pray for Mary's intercession with the joy of the Resurrection in your heart. Keep in your mind and heart the emotions that meditating on Jesus' Resurrection can bring you. Remember, it was only through Mary's yes that God's plan of salvation came into the world through the Resurrection of his Son.

has risen, as he said, alleluia

he said he would rise

Look closely at the gospel stories of Christ's Resurrection. The response of his disciples is very consistent. When they hear of the empty tomb, they respond in disbelief. When John arrives at the tomb, it takes seeing the burial cloths there to help him realize that what Jesus foretold has come true: he has risen from the dead. Before seeing the empty tomb with his own eyes, John's gospel tells us, John did not understand. Now, having seen, he believes (see Jn 20:2–9).

Thomas the Apostle has a similar experience. He misses Jesus' first appearance to the disciples and will not believe the others' testimony about his rising. He has to see Jesus himself to believe. Jesus says to him, and indirectly to us, that those who believe without having the opportunity to see him directly with their own eyes are blessed (see Jn 20:24–29).

Have you ever considered our belief in the Resurrection? We weren't there to see the Risen Lord. We can, however, place our trust in the testimony of the Apostles that has been passed down to us through scripture and tradition.

The other way to have faith in the Resurrection is to find the joy of God's presence at work in your life today. We may not be able to see God, but we can certainly see his work in the world if we are willing to let down our guard and trust that what he says is true.

meditation

Think about your own belief in the Resurrection for a moment. Where does your belief in the Resurrection find its foundation?

pray for us to god, alleluia

a praying queen

Let's compare for a moment the intercession we ask of Mary in the Angelus and the requests we place before her in the Regina Caeli. In the Angelus, we ask the Mother of God to pray that "we may be made worthy of the promises of Christ." In the Regina Caeli we are not as specific. After we ask Mary to rejoice early in the prayer, we ask her to pray for us. What would the joyful Mary ask for on our behalf? Undoubtedly that we will experience the same joy she has in heaven.

Later in the Regina Caeli, when we make our petition to God, we remind him of what we asked Mary to intercede for: that "we may obtain the joys of everlasting life." We may be blessed with joy in our lives today, but we also look ahead to the joys of our life with the Lord in heaven. This petition to God is not very different from the prayer request we set before Mary in the Angelus ("that we may be made worth of the promises of Christ"). Jesus promises us eternal joy in heaven even if we can never fully realize it in this life.

What a comfort this is! If we pray the Angelus and Regina Caeli on a daily basis, that means that Mary is asking her Son to grant us the joy in heaven each and every day. How exciting! With great expectation we can look forward to our future union with God and to the joy beyond all earthly joys.

meditation

Take a moment and feel comforted. Mary, the Mother of God, is praying for your joy today. She is there before God in heaven praying on your behalf. She wants you to experience the same joy that she experiences as Queen of Heaven. How could he turn down his mother? That joy is coming. Get ready.

rejoice and be glad, o virgin mary, alleluia

cultivating gladness

Think for a moment about the ways in which you have used the word "glad." We often say something like "I am glad x, y, and z happened." Or we might use the word in response to someone else's news, as in "Oh, I'm so glad to hear that."

Gladness is an emotion almost always expressed as a response. Something good happens, and we feel glad. It is slightly different from rejoicing because rejoicing requires an active posture. In the original Latin of the Regina Caeli, "be glad" is the translation of *gaude* while *gaudete* is translated as "rejoice." To rejoice is to do something active, while gladness is a state of being.

Why make the distinction? It is because we often choose, in response to certain events, not to be glad. Something happens in the world or to us, and we choose not to see the good in it. When we take some time to react to the events in our lives with gratitude, we can cultivate a state of gladness.

meditation

Spend some time today reflecting on everything that happened to you so far today. Offer gratitude to the Lord for these events. Choose to be glad even if you didn't think the day was as good as it could have been.

the virgin mary

With the invocation of Mary as virgin we recall in a small way the Angelus. Christ was conceived in Mary by the power of the Holy Spirit. According to Catholic Church teaching, Mary remained a virgin her entire life. Often, when we talk about Mary's virginity, we think of her purity—not purity in a rudimentary, she-never-had-sex sense, but purity in the sense of holiness before God. Mary was and is the supreme example of human holiness.

As we reflect on the Resurrection today while we pray the Regina Caeli, let us consider the ways in which God is calling us to be more holy. He continually calls us to be holy. He does not shame us for the unholy things we've done. Purity is a gift that he offers continuously. We have reason to rejoice and be glad because, just like the Virgin Mary, we are made holy by being filled with God's grace.

meditation

In which areas of your life has God made you holy? Instead of thinking of where you fall short, give thanks for the ways in which you have been made holy by the grace of God. In which situations or relationships in your life are you able to love with a self-giving love? In what ways are you already living out God's will?

for the lord has truly risen, alleluia

truly risen

Sometimes we have to say it to believe it: Jesus Christ died, but then he rose again. He died, but he came back to life. Like many things we profess as Christians, this belief can be easy to take for granted. We have heard about Jesus' rising so frequently in our lifetimes that we lose our sense of the outlandishness of the Resurrection. Jesus' coming back to life is highly unlikely and unbelievable. Even the apostles could not believe it for themselves.

In the Regina Caeli, we confirm our belief in the Resurrection two times, as if we are reassuring ourselves: yes, "the Lord has truly risen." As members of the Church community, we proclaim together Christ's rising from the dead. We have reason to join with Mary in rejoicing beyond belief that Christ is risen.

If we look closely at our Christian beliefs, not to doubt them but to appreciate them as gifts, they can be sources of great joy because behind every belief is a revelation of God's love for us. The Resurrection is proof of God's incredible love for us. He gives us the gift of new life. He gave us this gift through great suffering and death. We have every reason to frequently proclaim "alleluia" in response.

meditation

Think back to Lent and Holy Week: through his suffering, death, and Resurrection, Christ shows us God's infinite love and brings us incredible joy. With your Regina Caeli today, express gratitude to God for the gift of the Resurrection.

o god, who gave joy to the world through the resurrection of thy son, our lord jesus christ, grant, we beseech thee

the source of joy

We cannot force ourselves to feel joy. We can act as though we're happy and put a smile on our faces. Sometimes this can even give us a feeling of happiness. Joy, though, is different. It has to come from somewhere. Its source is outside—or deep inside—of us. We can search for and accept it, but we cannot fake it.

Joy is a gift from God that God gives us in many different ways. We can experience joy among family and friends, realizing how much we are loved by them and blessed by God. We can experience joy when encountering beauty in creation and we can experience joy in response to certain events.

The joy we proclaim in the Regina Caeli has its source in the Resurrection. God "gave joy to the world through the Resurrection." Even without the Resurrection, we would certainly have a lot to be thankful for:

God created us. He chose a special people to be his, and we are part of that people. He even became one of us to show us the path to joyful living. Ultimately, though, it is the Resurrection that is our true source of joy. Through the Resurrection, we can finally be fully united with the Lord and with his people. This is something that inspires true joy within us.

meditation

Imagine, for a moment, the joys of heaven: the experience of the Lord's perfect love and reunion with our lost loved ones. If you can, let the joy of the anticipation of heaven well up inside of you. Search for it. At the very least, give thanks to Jesus for the gift of new life through the Resurrection.

joy to the world

The hymn "Joy to the World" is traditionally, of course, a Christmas carol. We don't often think of it during the season of Easter, but it certainly expresses the same sentiment as the Regina Caeli. Just as we repeated the sounding joy of Jesus' birth, so, too, can we proclaim joy to the world during this season of Easter. God gave joy to the world through the Resurrection of Christ.

The words of the song are based on Psalm 98, which encourages the reader to sing praise and shout with joy to the Lord. If you read this psalm closely, you can't help but think of the Resurrection with every verse. The words sing of marvelous deeds, victory, all the ends of the earth, rivers, mountains, justice, fairness, and governance—all of which take on new meaning in light of the Resurrection.

As we continue to pray this wonderful prayer

and meditate on the meaning of the Resurrection, let us take moments throughout our day to appreciate what God has done. Let us not stop at speaking our thanks to God; let us give him the full song of praise that he really deserves.

meditation

Pick your favorite verse from the Christmas carol "Joy to the World." Sing it in your head, but think of the Resurrection instead of the birth of Christ. Make the words of the song your words as you praise God for the gift of the Resurrection.

that through the
intercession of the
virgin mary, his
mother

intercessory prayer

Will you pray for me? I mean it. Please, say a prayer for the author of this book. I would really appreciate it. To be able to pray to God on behalf of someone is an incredible gift and an amazing responsibility.

Each time we pray the Regina Caeli we ask that Mary pray for us. Why? What do we hope her prayers will do for us? We hope to experience the joys of everlasting life. These are the same joys that Mary herself is experiencing right now. She doesn't share that joy with us directly but asks God to bestow it upon us. We are united in joy through intercessory prayer.

Back to my prayer request. When you pray for me and I pray for you—and I am praying for you as I write this—we are united together. That same joy of everlasting life is made manifest through our mutual concern for one another. When I know someone is praying for me, it gives me hope. It makes me smile. I experience a sense of joy.

Thank you for your prayers.

meditation

Ask someone to pray for you today. We are not afraid to ask Mary to pray for us each time we pray the Regina Caeli. Let's keep going. Ask a friend or family member to pray for you and promise to pray for them in return. Those prayers unite you together in love and hope for the joy of everlasting life.

mother of mercy

In the Hail Holy Queen, another Catholic prayer highlighting the royalty of Mary, we call her the "Mother of Mercy." I love that title. Mary is the Mother of Jesus, in whom we find infinite mercy. She is, therefore, the Mother of Mercy. Our shame and guilt are healed through the mercy of God. In him we find love, unity, and hope for our future.

Mary, who is full of grace, is also full of mercy. She intercedes for us not only because we ask but because of her overwhelming desire to be merciful. Inspired by her relationship with her son, she pours out her prayers on our behalf. She wants us to know the same mercy she knows so well as the Mother of God.

This is what mercy compels us to do: filled with the joy of God's mercy, we go out and extend mercy to others. We help and listen and serve wherever we are needed. Through that mercy, others come to know Christ in deeper ways, too, and get to experience mercy directly from him themselves.

meditation

When you ask the Holy Queen, Mother of Mercy, to pray for you today, focus in a special way on God's merciful, healing love. Ask that his mercy be extended to you and to anyone you know who in a particular way needs that mercy today. If you can, be a vessel of that mercy by reaching out to that person.

we may obtain the joys of everlasting life

having more hope

Is our anticipation of the joys of everlasting life limited? Are we truly able to grasp the depth of joy that heaven will provide? People always say that you can't really know what heaven will be like, but they can list for you metaphors, feelings, and thoughts about what God has in store for us—things that they hope for.

As Christians, we believe that the joy of everlasting life is truly beyond measure. It is a mystery to be unfolded before us. Quite possibly, our hope and anticipation are too small. We often associate heaven with images of clouds, golden gates, trumpets, angels, and people walking around in white garments. While these images can be helpful, they are too small. We need to have hope in something much, much greater. Praying the Regina Caeli each day can help us broaden our horizon of hope in the joys of everlasting life.

meditation

Think of the most joyful moment of your life. Now imagine an even more joyful experience. Can you do it? Pretty difficult, huh? Recognizing that the joys of everlasting life are far beyond our comprehension, let us turn to God in hope and gratitude for the amazing gift he has in store for us.

feel the flow

The "flow state" is a concept coined by psychologist Mihaly Csikszentmihalyi in his research and in his book, *Flow*. Athletes call it "being in the zone." You experience it when you are so engaged in an activity that time seems to stand still; your consciousness seems to exist almost outside of time. Many people who experience this flow state begin to crave it. They try desperately to recreate it at every possible opportunity. Why? Because the experience of flow is the experience of joy.

Joy is not happiness. Joy comes with the feeling of peacefulness that is present also in the flow state. When we are in the zone, we connect with our true selves. We are doing the work that we love and able to act without any consciousness of the world around us. It is easy to question ourselves and doubt our abilities. We struggle to achieve some goal or carry out some task, and the frustration takes a physical toll on us. When we are in a flow state, though, we are at peace—a peace that feels like joy.

I have a hunch that the joys of everlasting life will be a lot like flow. Just as people report feeling as though they were outside of time while in the zone, so too will we be outside of time in heaven. Our everlasting life won't feel long at all; instead, we will feel like we're in the zone without being bogged down by time.

meditation

Have you ever experienced the flow state? What was that experience like? Would you call it joy? How do you think that experience might compare to the joys of everlasting life?

the joy of a saint

Have you ever wondered if heaven might get boring? For something to be everlasting means it will never end. Sure, we will have everything we could possibly want. The people we love will be there. Things will be amazing—never better. Yet, the idea of doing the same thing for "everlasting" time can be difficult to understand as joyful.

This is because seeking something different is our default perspective. We pursue things that are different and better. This affinity for growth keeps us interested, engaged, motivated, and excited. We look for better jobs, better homes, better cars, better stuff, and an all-around better way of life. But if we always strive for the better, and if in heaven there is nothing "better," how can we be happy?

As Christians, we place our hope in God, trusting that one day we will be united with him and all his children in everlasting life. I do not know what everlasting life will be like, but I do know that we will be filled with the joys of everlasting life and we won't be bored. I suspect that joy is possible in eternity only insofar as we are able to be satisfied with what we have on earth rather than constantly seeking something better.

Regardless of what heaven is like, we do know what we will be like. We will be saints and we will be filled with everlasting joy. We will be people so devoid of selfishness that our only desires will be to be with God, to please God, and to share his love with others. That's joy—the joy of a saint.

I daresay that we don't have to be in heaven to experience this joy. If we truly want to prepare for the joys of everlasting life, it is time to start living like a saint now. Instead of constantly pursuing the "better," let us be joyful with and grateful for what we have.

meditation

Examine your personal desires for something better than what you have. Have you convinced yourself that you can experience joy only after fulfilling that desire? As you pray today, consider how you might find joy regardless of what you have: the job, house, stuff, and people in your life. Experiencing the joy of everlasting life doesn't have to wait until after death. We can start to experience it right now if we are open to it as a gift from Christ our Lord.

angelus (latin)

V. Angelus Domini nuntiavit Mariae.
R. Et concepit de Spiritu Sancto.
Ave Maria, gratia plena; Dominus tecum: benedicta
tu in mulieribus, et benedictus fructus ventris tui
Iesus. Sancta Maria, Mater Dei ora pro nobis
peccatoribus, nunc et in hora mortis nostrae. Amen.

V. Ecce ancilla Domini,
R. Fiat mihi secundum verbum tuum.
Ave Maria. . .

V. Et Verbum caro factum est,
R. Et habitavit in nobis.
Ave Maria. . .

V. Ora pro nobis, sancta Dei Genetrix,
R. Ut digni efficiamur promissionibus Christi.

Oremus.
Gratiam tuam, quaesumus, Domine, mentibus
nostris infunde; ut qui, Angelo nuntiante, Christi
Filii tui incarnationem cognovimus, per passionem
eius et crucem ad resurrectionis gloriam
perducamur. Per eumdem Christum Dominum
nostrum.
Amen.

regina caeli (latin)

Regina coeli, laetare, alleluia.
Quia quem meruisti portare, alleluia.

Resurrexit sicut dixit, alleluia.
Ora pro nobis Deum, alleluia.

V. Gaude et laetare, Virgo Maria, Alleluia,
R. Quia surrexit Dominus vere, alleluia.

Oremus
Deus qui per resurrectionem Filii tui, Domini nostri
Iesu Christi, mundum laetificare dignatus es:
praesta, quaesumus, ut per eius Genetricem
Virginem Mariam, perpetuae capiamus gaudia vitae.
Per eundem Christum Dominum nostrum.
Amen.

notes

1. Benedict XVI, "On the Word of God in the Life and Mission of the Church," Apostolic Exhortation *Verbum Domini* (Vatican City: Libreria Editrice Vaticana, 2010), 88, http://w2.vatican.va/content/benedict-xvi/en/apost_exhortations/documents/hf_ben-xvi_ exh_20100930_verbum-domini.html.

2. Irenaeus, *Against Heresies*, Book III, 22:4.

3. John Donne, "Meditation XVII," *Devotions upon Emergent Occasions*, http://www.online-literature.com/donne/409/.

4. Francis, Twitter post, June 3, 2013, 3:05 a.m., https://twitter.com/Pontifex.

5. John Paul II, Angelus address, March 4, 1979 (Vatican City: Libreria Editrice Vaticana, 1979), 1, https://w2.vatican.va/content/ john-paul-ii/en/angelus/1979/documents/hf_jp-ii_ang_19790304.html.

6. *The Usual Suspects*, directed by Bryan Singer (1995; Beverly Hills, CA: MGM Studios).

7. C. S. Lewis, *The Screwtape Letters* (San Francisco: HarperOne, 2001), xx.

about the author

JARED DEES is the creator of The Religion Teacher (TheReligionTeacher.com), a popular website that provides practical resources and teaching strategies to religious educators. A respected graduate of the Alliance for Catholic Education (ACE) program at the University of Notre Dame, Dees holds master's degrees in education and theology, both from Notre Dame. He frequently gives keynotes and leads workshops at conferences, church events, and school in-services throughout the year on a variety of topics. He lives near South Bend, Indiana, with his wife and children.

Learn more about Jared's books, speaking events, and other projects at jareddees.com.

also by jared dees

Made in United States
Troutdale, OR
12/27/2023

16461455R00116